LiBEARy Skills

(Kindergarten through Grade Three)

By
The School Librarians of
Chambersburg, Pennsylvania

Cynthia Drawbaugh
Delores Boggs
Joan Bowen
Susanne Detrich
Darlene Miley
Elizabeth Renshaw
Jean Rieck
Sharon Sheffler
Patricia Sweeney

Cover and inside page illustrations by
Jennifer Ellis

Publishers
T.S. Denison and Company, Inc.
Minneapolis, MN 55431

1

Standard Book Number: 513-02043-8
LiBEARy Skills – Kindergarten through Grade Three
Copyright © 1990 by the T. S. Denison & Co., Inc.
Minneapolis, Minnesota 55431

Table of Contents

Introduction

A Breakthrough in Library Instruction –
Educational, Easy and Enchanting!

LiBEARy, the library bears present library skills to students in grades K-3. This reproducible book is a planned course of study for each grade level. Poetry, fingerplays, art projects, and an abundant variety of activities are also included in this very special new resource. Task sheets are used to teach book care rules, parts of a book, arrangements of books, dictionary skills, reference skills and more! Superb illustrations add great warmth to this wonderful material!

KINDERGARTEN LIBRARY SKILLS

LiBEARy
Learns
About
The
Library

Table of Contents
Kindergarten

THE LIBRARY

I love the library
(hug body)
It's my favorite place.
Rows of books in every case.
*(With palms together to represent a
closed book, open arms slowly)*

Fat books --
(Arms Forward to make a fat circle)
Thin books --
(Palms flat against tummy)
From wall to wall --
(Move hands to left and then to the right)

If I read and read, I'll read them all.
(Open palms together to represent an open book)

Unknown

Name _____ Grade _____

Please color me. If you would like to, cut me out, glue a popsicle stick or straw to my back, and I'll be your puppet.

Dear Parents,

Today your child brought home a library book for the first time. We have been talking about taking care of our books and finding a safe place to keep our books so your child may ask for some suggestions.

Thank you for your help in encouraging your child to use our library. I hope your child enjoys visiting the library and if you're ever near by, stop in and visit. We think there's a lot happening at our school library.

Name _____ Grade _____

Get on the Library Train

Color your face on the library train.

Name _____ Grade _____

1. Color the shelf marker.

2. Print your name on the line.

3. Cut on the dotted line.

Note to teacher:
Mount on oaktag and laminate.
Markers can be used to mark
place on shelf during book selection.

NAME

**LiBEARy says,
"Be sure to sign your name
in the beary first
empty space."**

Se		D23,329
Seuss, Dr.		
AUTHOR		
Hop on pop		
TITLE		
		1-2
	♡	

Name _____ Grade _____

When you come to the library -

Walk real fine
In a nice, straight line.

How does your teacher look when you do this?

Name _____ Grade _____

When you visit the library -

Dance and shout
And Jump about.

How does your librarian look when you do this?

Name _____ Grade _____

Don't touch your friends. That is wrong.
Keep your hands where they belong.

How does your teacher look when you do this?

Name _____ Grade _____

When a story is being read,
Lie down like you're in bed.

How does your teacher look when you do this?

Name _____ Grade _____

When you visit the library -

With a friendly look,
Share a book.

How does your teacher look when you do this?

LiBEARy knows that when he is finished looking at his book, he should mark his place with a bookmark. He never uses anything thicker than a piece of paper to mark his place. He knows that anything else could break the spine of the book.

This is LiBEARy's book with a bookmark in it, ready to mark the place where he stopped reading. Color the bookmark red.

LiBEARy knows that before he touches a book he needs to check his hands. He wants to make sure that he has clean hands because dirt could ruin the pages of his library book.

We need some things to help us make sure that our hands are clean. Circle the things below that could help make sure that your hands are clean before you touch your library book.

LiBEARy is so unhappy. He just found a library book that he really wanted to read, but look what he found when he opened the book. Someone who didn't know how to treat a book wrote all over the pages. No one likes to look at a book when someone has scribbled all over the pages. LiBEARy knows never to write in a library book.

Look at the two books below. Circle the book that shows the way a library book should look. Draw an "X" over the book that would make LiBEARy unhappy.

LiBEARy is so unhappy. He chose a new library book and when he opened it he found that someone had cut a big hole in several of the pages. LiBEARy knows that there are several things we should never use on a library book. We never cut out pages of a book.

Here are some things. Put an "X" over the things that we should never use on a book.

LiBEARy loves to take a bath but he knows that a library book can't stand to take a bath. We must be very careful never to let our books get wet.

One way to protect our books when it is raining or wet outside is to carry them in a plastic bag or book bag. Here is an empty book bag. Draw your library book inside the bag.

LiBEARy was looking at his library book and found that someone turned down the corner of the page to mark their place in the book. LiBEARy knows that the best way to mark your place is with a bookmark.

Look at the two books below. Draw a circle around the book that has been marked the right way.

LiBEARy loves to enjoy a sandwich and a nice glass of milk. He knows that his library books don't enjoy a snack. He is very careful to keep his books far away from his food. He never offers his books a sandwich.

LiBEARy's book never has to worry about having a sandwich stuck to its pages. Circle the picture that shows how this makes his book feel.

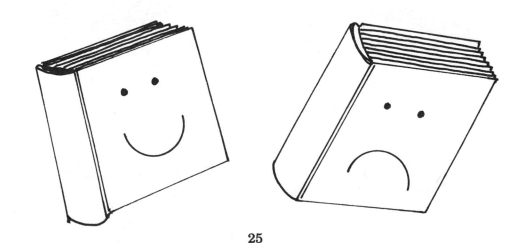

LiBEARy just got home and look what he found. His dog, Page, just ate his library book for his after school snack. LiBEARy is so careful to keep his books in a safe place because he knows that puppies don't know how to treat books. Draw some books on LiBEARy's bookshelf because this would be a good place to keep a book.

Circle the picture that shows how a book feels when a puppy uses it for a snack.

LiBEARy opened his library book and he found that someone had punched little holes on one of the pages. He knows that we must always be very careful when we use something that might make a hole in a book.

Put an "X" over the things that we should not use around a book.

LiBEARy loves to read new books so he always returns his books right on time. He knows that he can get a new book each time he returns his old book. He also knows that other people might be waiting to read his book.

Fill in the blank below with the time that you visit the library. See if you can remember to return your book on time.

I visit the library on _____

LiBEARy loves to share reading a book with his baby sister but he knows that little babies don't always know how to treat a book. He is always very careful to put his book away in a safe place after they are finished reading.

On the back of this paper draw a picture of a safe place where you can keep your book away from baby brothers and sisters.

LiBEARy was reading his library book when he found a torn page. Whenever we find a torn page we shoud never try to fix it. Always give the book to the librarian so she can mend the book with a special tape.

Name _____ Grade _____

Help LiBEARy remember the beary best way to treat his library books. Circle each picture that shows a good way to treat books.

Name _____ Grade _____

Connect the dots in alphabetical order.

Name _____ Grade _____

Directions: Circle the picture which finishes the
              sentence correctly.

The title of this book is

The author uses

The illustrator uses

Name _____ Grade _____

Directions: Circle the picture which matches the words.

The spine of the book

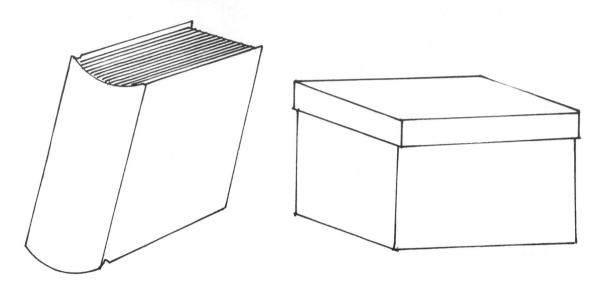

The book cover

GRADE ONE LIBRARY SKILLS

**Bounce
Into The Library
With
LiBEARy**

Table of Contents
Grade One

Name _____ Grade _____

I am sitting in the library with my friends and our librarian. The name of our librarian is_____. I am sitting next to her.

**SHELF
MARKER**

**SHELF
MARKER**

**SHELF
MARKER**

Name _____

LiBEARy
knows that every
book in our library
has its own place
on the shelf.
He uses a shelf
marker so he knows where
to replace his book.

Circle each book that is on the
shelf the wrong way.

Add books to this bookcase the
right way.

Name _____

Circle the bookcase that makes LiBEARy happy.

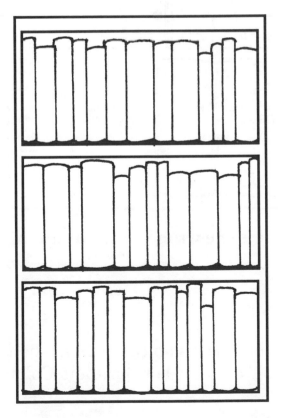 

Name _____

This is a bookcase from our library. How many shelves does it have?

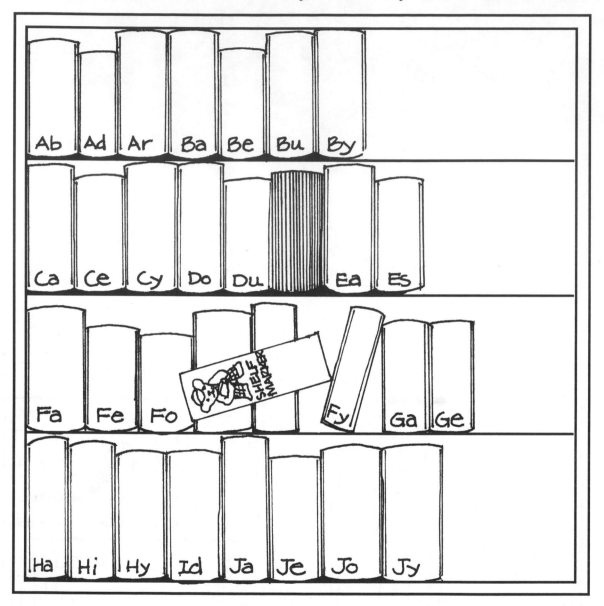

Find the book on the second shelf that is the wrong way. Put an "X" over it.

Find the shelf marker. Color it green.

Color 3 books on the top shelf red. Color 2 books on the bottom shelf yellow. Find the book that has a capital "I" on the bottom shelf. Color it blue.

Name _____ Grade _____

LiBEARy says,
"Be sure and sign your name
in the beary first
empty space."

	D23,329
Se Seuss, Dr.	
AUTHOR	
Hop on pop	
TITLE	1-2

	♡	

	BORROWER'S NAME	
	♡	

Name _____ Grade _____

LiBEARy is returning his book on time. I must return my book in
_____ week.

Name _____ Grade _____

Book Care Rules

Draw a line from the picture to the book care rule.

Put books on a bookshelf away from small brothers and sisters and pets.

Never write or scribble in a book.

Always have clean hands before touching a book.

Always turn pages from the upper right corner.

Book Care Bookmarks

LiBEARy says, "Always keep your book dry."

LiBEARy's Best Bookcare Rules

LiBEARy says, "Turn the pages of a book from the upper right corner."

LiBEARy's Best Bookcare Rules

LiBEARy says, "Always have clean hands before touching a book."

LiBEARy's Best Bookcare Rules

LiBEARy says, "Never write or scribble on a book."

LiBEARy's Best Bookcare Rules

LiBEARy says, "Keep books on a bookshelf or in a safe place."

LiBEARy's Best Bookcare Rules

Name _____ Grade _____

Fiction Books

Some books have stories that were made up by a person called an author. These books never happened except in the author's mind. They are imaginary. We call these books fiction books.

Is this bear fiction or nonfiction? Circle the correct word.

Name _____ Grade _____

Fiction Bear

Write the word fiction under the make believe bear.

_____

_____

Name _____ Grade _____

Berenstain Bears

Jan and Stan Berenstain write the books about the Berenstain Bears. To find the books they have written on the library shelves, you need to find the first two letters of their last name. Those letters are called author letters. Down below circle the author letters.

The Bike Lesson

by

Stan and Jan Berenstain

BEGINNER BOOKS A Division of Random House, Inc.

Name _____ Grade _____

This book is open to the title page of the book. This page is usually the second or third page in the book. Often it has a picture from the book. It will tell you the title of the book and the name of the author. Find the title on this title page and draw a red circle around it. Find the name of the author and underline the name with a blue crayon.

What's the Matter with

CARRUTHERS?

A Bedtime Story

written and illustrated by

JAMES MARSHALL

HOUGHTON MIFFLIN COMPANY BOSTON

Nonfiction Books

Some books have information in them called facts. We call these books nonfiction books. An example of a nonfiction book would be how to take care of a dog. Certain facts are given on how the dog must be cared for.

Is this dog fiction or nonfiction? Circle the correct word.

Name _____ Grade _____

Fiction or Nonfiction

Is this picture fiction or nonfiction? Circle the correct word.

Name _____ Grade _____

This book is open to the title page of a nonfiction book. The title page is usually the second or third page in the book. It sometimes has a picture from the book. It will also tell you the title of the book and the name of the author.

Find the title of the book on the title page and circle it in red. Find the name of the author and circle it in blue.

MINNESOTA:

Its People and Culture

By

W. E. ROSENFELT

Publishers

T. S. DENISON & COMPANY, INC.

Minneapolis

Name _____ Grade _____

Nonfiction books are books that have facts. Fiction books are imaginary stories. Sometimes by looking at the pictures we can decide if a book is fiction or nonfiction.

Look at the pictures below. Decide which picture would be found in a nonfiction book and which picture would be found in a fiction book. Circle each picture that you think would be found in a fiction book.

OR

OR

OR

*From *McElligot's Pool* by Dr. Seuss.
Copyright © 1947 by Random House, Inc.
Copyright renewed © 1974 by Theodor S. Geisel and Audrey S. Geisel.
Reprinted by permission of Random House, Inc.

Name _____ Grade _____

What happened first?

In the story Goldilocks and the Three Bears, what was the first thing that happened? Find the picture that shows that below and put a 1 in the space at the bottom of the picture. See if you can number each picture in the order in which it happened.

LiBEARy has a real problem. He recognizes all these words from the library but they're supposed to be in alphabetical order. Can you help him arrange his list in alphabetical order? Find the word that would come first and write it next to the number. Continue until you have used all the words and LiBEARy will have his list in order.

NONFICTION	1. _____
BOOK	2. _____
TITLE	3. _____
LIBRARY	4. _____
AUTHOR	5. _____
COVER	6. _____
FICTION	7. _____
SPINE	8. _____

Name _____ Grade _____

This is a special library friend.
Connect the dots to see who is looking at you.

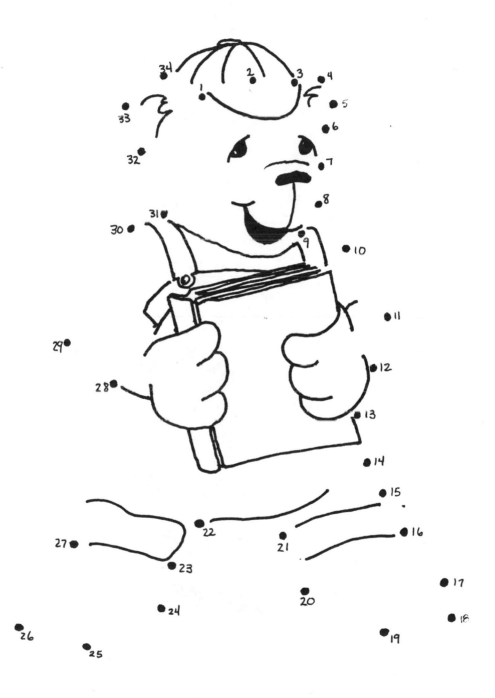

57

Name _____ Grade _____

There is one thing that LiBEARy loves. Can you guess what it is? Connect the dots and you will find a picture of one of LiBEARy's favorite things.

A Bear On the Farm

By Bearington Bearmore

58

Name _____ Grade _____

Connect the dots to look at one of our library friends.
Then connect the numbers to see what he is holding.

HOW A BOOK IS PUT ON THE SHELF

When you look at the bottom of the spine of a fiction book, you should see two letters. These letters tell you where the book belongs on the shelf. Since fiction books have only letters they are always arranged in alphabetical order.

Someone left a stack of fiction books that need to be put away on the bookshelf. Can you find the book that would come first and write the letters in the first book on the shelf. Fill in all the books in the correct order.

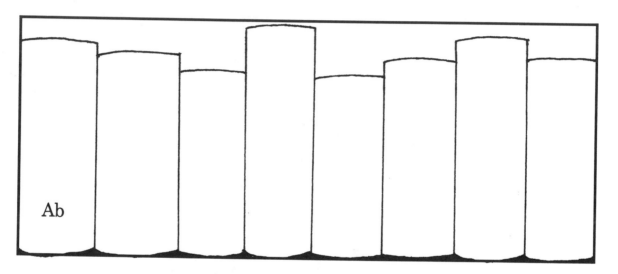

Li-bear-ry has already done the first one for you. Now see if you can fill in the rest of the books.

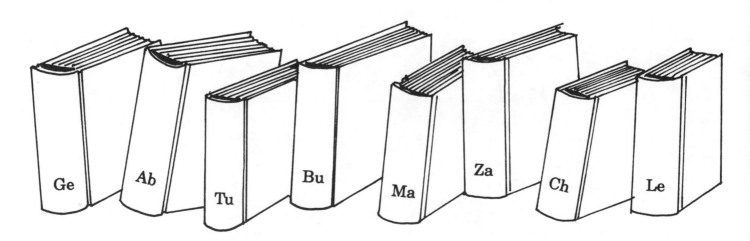

Name _____ Grade _____

An encyclopedia is a special set of books in a library. We can look up many different things in an encyclopedia.

Choose an animal. Find a picture of that animal in the encyclopedia. Draw a picture of the animal in the middle of this page.

Name of animal _____

Write one thing about the animal.

_____

_____

_____

GRADE TWO LIBRARY SKILLS

LiBEARy
Explores
The
Library

Table of Contents
Grade Two

What is a Book?
by
Lora Dunetz

A book is pages, pictures, and words;
A book is animals, people, and birds;
A book is stories of queens and kings,
Poems, and songs - so many things!
Curled in a corner where I can hide,
With a book I can journey far and wide.
Though it's only paper from end to end,
A book is a very special friend.

INTRODUCTION TO SHELVES

Each book in a library has its own place on a shelf.
One kind of book is kept in place by two letters; a capital letter and a small letter. These books are storybooks.

Al	Be	Co	Di	Ea	Fl	Ga	Ho	Is	Jo

The other kind of book is kept in place by numbers with letters. These books are about real things.

031 Wa	170 St	221 Ba	394 Pe	423 Ea	551 Cl	636 He	741 Am	811 He	921 Jo

You can find your own special book by using the alphabet and counting when you know where to look.

COVERS AND SPINES

The cover of a book protects its pages.
The spine of a book holds it together.
You can usually find the title of the book in both places.

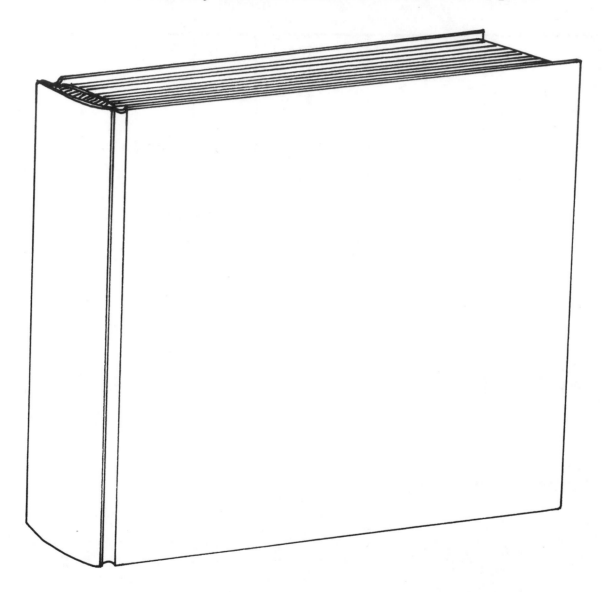

Use one of the books you selected today.
Put the title on the cover and on the spine in this picture.
Draw a picture on the cover and decorate the spine.

TITLE PAGE

The title page is found at the beginning of a book.
The title page tells you what the book is called, who wrote it, and who made the pictures.

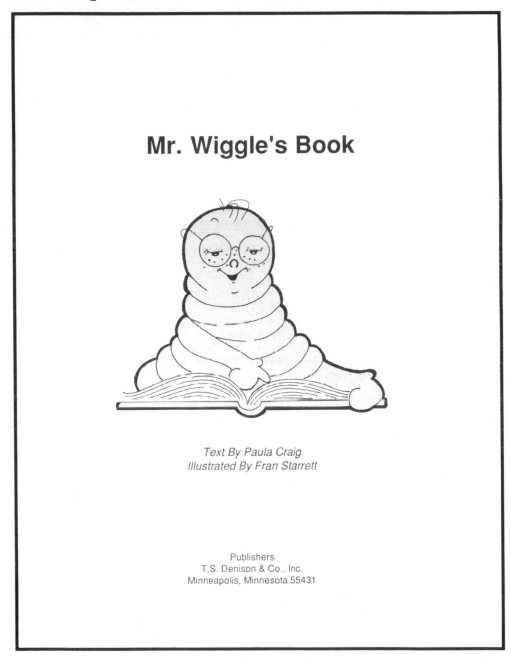

Show the librarian the title page of a book you selected.

Name _____ Grade _____

Use the title page of the book to find the title.
Write the title of the books you selected.

_____
Title

_____
Title

- -

Name _____ Grade _____

Use the title page of the book to find the title.
Write the title of the books you selected.

_____
Title

_____
Title

AUTHORS

An author is a person who writes a book.

The author has something to say to the reader and says it with the words of the book.

You can find the author's name in your book by using some word clues.

Some clue words are

By
Story by
Written by
Told by
Retold by
Selected by
Compiled by
Text by
or
Just the author's name

Be sure to read your books to find what the author wants to say to you.

Name _____ Grade _____

Use the title page of the book to find the title and author.
Write them on the proper lines.

_____
Title

_____
Author

- -

Name _____ Grade _____

Use the title page of the book to find the title and author.
Write them on the proper lines.

_____
Title

_____
Author

ILLUSTRATOR

An illustrator is a person who makes the pictures for a book. The pictures are called illustrations.

The illustrator tries to show with illustrations what the author is saying. Sometimes the author and illustrator are the same person.

You can find the illustrator's name in your book by using some clue words.

Some clue words are
Pictures by
Illustrated by
Story and pictures by
Written and illustrated by
Drawings by
Photos by

Be sure to enjoy the illustrations in the books you read.

Name _____ Grade _____

Use the title page of the book to find the title, author and illustrator.
Write them on the proper lines.

_____
Title

_____
Author

_____
Illustrator

- -

Name _____ Grade _____

Use the title page of the book to find the title, author and illustrator.
Write them on the proper lines.

_____
Title

_____
Author

_____
Illustrator

KINDS OF BOOKS

There are two kinds of books in a library. They are fiction and nonfiction.

Fiction books are made-up, imaginary stories.
Nonfiction books give information and facts.

Which bear would be in a fiction book? Color it.

Select one fiction book today that has an imaginary animal in the story.

KINDS OF BOOKS

Nonfiction books give factual information about real things.

Which bear would you find in a nonfiction book. Color it.

Select one nonfiction book today that has information in it about a real animal.

KINDS OF BOOKS

Nursery rhymes and fairy tales are stories from long, long ago. They have a special place with nonfiction books.

What story have these bears in it?

Select one fairy tale book today.

Name _____ Grade _____

Find this fiction book on the shelf. Put this paper in it and put it at the collection place.

_____   _____
Call Number   Title

- -

Name _____ Grade _____

Find this fiction book on the shelf. Put this paper in it and put it at the collection place.

_____   _____
Call Number   Title

- -

Name _____ Grade _____

Find this fiction book on the shelf. Put this paper in it and put it at the collection place.

_____   _____
Call Number   Title

ARRANGEMENT OF FICTION

Fiction books are placed on the shelf by the first 3 letters of the author's name.

Below are some fiction books that need to be put back on the shelves. Look at the call numbers. Put the call numbers in order on the right shelf.

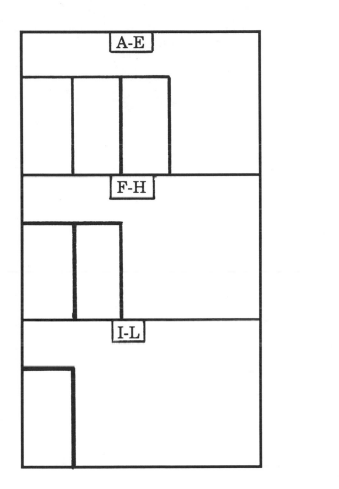

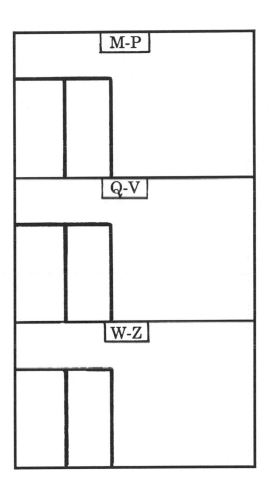

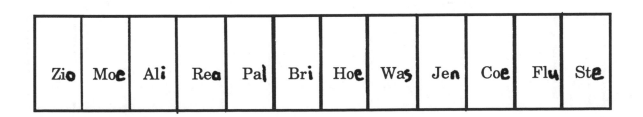

When the first letters are the same, you need to look at the second letter of the authors' names. Draw the books at the bottom of the page on the bookshelf in alphabetical order.

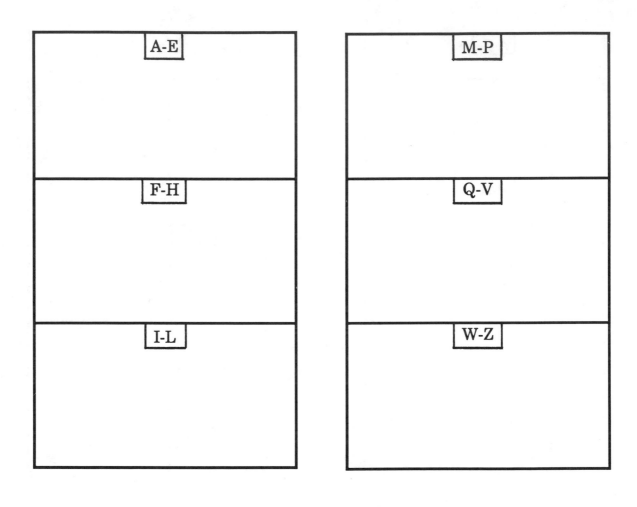

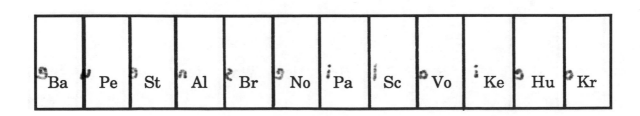

ARRANGEMENT OF NON-FICTION

Here are the shelves for the non-fiction books. Can you put the books in the right order on the shelves? Draw the books on the shelves in the correct number order and put the call numbers on the spine.

000-200	700
300-400	800
500-600	900

921 Li	811 Ke	568 Sh	028 Be	636 He	920 An	398 Pa	423 Ea	817 Ro	234 St	133 Co	796 Ra

CARD CATALOG

The library has a set of drawers called a Card Catalog. Each drawer holds a lot of cards. The cards have the name of the author, title, and call number. These cards are in alphabetical order.

Below is a picture of a card catalog. Fill in the missing letters.

A - C	K - M	S - U
D - F	N - P	V - X
G - J	Q - R	Y - Z

A - C _____ K - M _____ S - U _____

D - F _____ N - P _____ V - X _____

G - J _____ Q - R _____ Y - Z _____

CARD CATALOG

You can be an explorer in the library and find a book for yourself. You can do this by using the card catalog.

A - C	K - M	S - U
D - F	N - P	V - X
G - J	Q - R	Y - Z

This is a sample of a card catalog. Here are three clues you can use to find a book you would like to read.

Call number   Pa   Amelia Badeli   Title

by Peggy Parrish

Grade level   Gr. 1-2

When you have found the book you want in the card catalog, then you must decide if it is fiction or nonfiction.

Name _____ Grade _____

Choose a book from the card catalog to locate in the library.

_____   _____
Call Number   Title

_____   _____
Fiction or Nonfiction   Grade Level

- -

Name _____ Grade _____

Choose a book from the card catalog to locate in the library.

_____   _____
Call Number   Title

_____   _____
Fiction or Nonfiction   Grade Level

- -

Name _____ Grade _____

Choose a book from the card catalog to locate in the library.

_____   _____
Call Number   Title

_____   _____
Fiction or Nonfiction   Grade Level

EXPLORING THE DICTIONARY

A dictionary is an alphabetical list of words and what they mean. It also shows you how to say the word, how to use the word in a sentence, and sometimes the dictionary shows a picture of the word.

A dictionary can be a book by itself, or it can be part of a book.

Below is a sample of a dictionary page. Find the word **bear**. Put an "X" over the pronunciation for the word. Color the picture of the balloon. Underline the sentence for baseball. Circle the meaning for the word **believe**.

bake   beach   bear   bell

bake (bak) To cook in an oven. Mom will bake a cake.

balloon (bal-loon) A toy made of thin rubber that you can blow up with air. I bought a baloon at the circus.

barn (bärn) A building on a farm. The cows are in the barn.

baseball (bas-bal) A game played with a ball and a bat. A baseball team has nine players.

beach (bech) Land next to water. My family goes to the beach in the summer.

bear (bar) A large shaggy animal. The bear ran out of the woods.

bedtime (bed-tim) The time you go to sleep. My bedtime is 9:00.

believe (be-leve) To think something is true. I believe the story in the book.

bell (bel) Something that rings. Did you hear the school bell ring?

USING GUIDE WORDS

At the top of a dictionary page are guide words. They help you find the words you want much faster. The guide words tell you the first and last word on that page.

Use the Guide Words from the dictionary in the back of your Spelling book or your classroom dictionary to find these words. If the words are not in your Spelling book decide where they would be found using the guide words. Write the guide words on the line under the word.

desert   spring

_____   _____

bike   Friday

_____   _____

nickel   whiskers

_____   _____

zoo   anything

_____   _____

circus   dinosaur

_____   _____

MY FAVORITE BOOKS

Call Number   Title

1. _____   _____

2. _____   _____

3. _____   _____

4. _____   _____

5. _____   _____

6. _____   _____

7. _____   _____

8. _____   _____

9. _____   _____

10. _____   _____

GRADE THREE LIBRARY SKILLS

LiBEARy
Introduces
the Bear Necessities
for the Library

Table of Contents
Grade Three

BOOK CARE

Our Books

Our books are our companions
    We love them and we need them,
We learn a million things from books,
    And that is why we read them.

So turn their pages carefully
    Don't crumple them or fold them.
Don't smear or smudge, or tear your books
    Or crush them while you hold them.

Remember to respect your books
    For in them you will find
The precious thoughts and feelings of
    Some person's heart and mind!

Treat all your books with loving care
    While on or off your shelf.
Regard them as kind neighbors,
    And love them as yourself!

10 Tips for Choosing a Book!

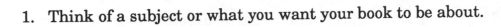

1. Think of a subject or what you want your book to be about.

2. Decide if you would like fiction or nonfiction.

3. Look for a special title.

4. Look for an author friend you know.

5. Share books with your friends and listen to what they say about their books.

6. Look at library displays.

7. Get up your courage to try something new.

8. Use a booklist.

9. Choose an award list.

10. Take the librarian's recommendation.

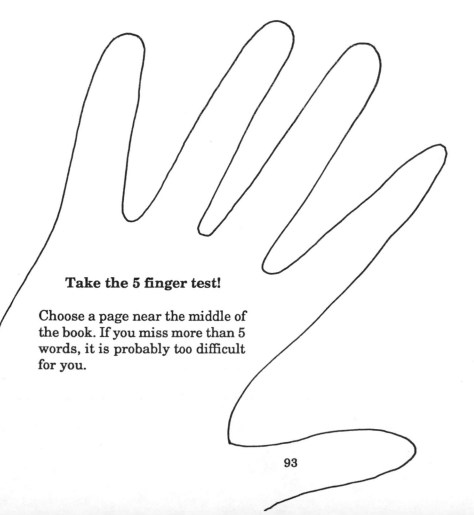

Take the 5 finger test!

Choose a page near the middle of the book. If you miss more than 5 words, it is probably too difficult for you.

CALDECOTT AWARD BOOKS

An award is given each year to the best illustrated children's book. It is called the Caldecott Medal. It is named after Randolph Caldecott, an English illustrator of children's books.

On the next three pages you will find listed all the Caldecott Award Books since 1938. We do not have all these books in our library.

The Caldecott Award Medal looks like this:

Front

Back

- -

Name _____ Grade _____

CALDECOTT AWARD BOOK

This is an award winning book I have read.

Title _____

Author _____

Illustrator _____

CALDECOTT AWARD BOOKS

Year	Title	Illustrator	Call Number
1938	*Animals of the Bible*	Dorothy Lathrop	(220 Bi)
1939	*Mei Li*	Thomas Handforth	(Ha)
1940	*Abraham Lincoln*	Ingri and Edgar Parin d'Aulaire	(921 Li)
1941	*They Were Strong and Good*	Robert Lawson	(920 La)
1942	*Make Way for Ducklings*	Robert McCloskey	(McC)
1943	*The Little House*	Virginia Lee Burton	(Bu)
1944	*Many Moons*	Louis Slobodkin	(Th)
1945	*A Prayer for a Child*	Elizabeth Orton Jones	(264 Fi)
1946	*The Rooster Crows*	Maud and Miska Petersham	(811.08 Pe)
1947	*The Little Island*	Leonard Weisgard	(MacD)
1948	*White Snow, Bright Snow*	Roger Duvoisin	(Tr)
1949	*The Big Snow*	Berta and Elmer Hader	(Ha)
1950	*Song of the Swallows*	Leo Politi	(Po)
1951	*The Egg Tree*	Katherine Milhouse	(Mi)
1952	*Finders Keepers*	Nicolas Mordvinoff	(Wi)
1953	*The Biggest Bear*	Lynd Ward	(Wa)
1954	*Madeline's Rescue*	Ludwig Bemelmans	(Be)

CALDECOTT AWARD BOOKS

Year	Title	Illustrator	Call Number
1955	*Cinderella*	Marcia Brown	(398.2 Pe)
1956	*Frog Went A-Courtin'*	Fedor Rojankovsky	(821 La)
1957	*A Tree Is Nice*	Marc Simont	(582 Ud)
1958	*Time of Wonder*	Robert McCloskey	(917.41 McC)
1959	*Chanticleer and the Fox*	Barbara Cooney	(821 Co)
1960	*Nine Days to Christmas*	Marie Hall Ets and Aurora Labastida	(Et)
1961	*Babouska and the Three Kings*	Niclosa Sidjakov	(398.2 Ro)
1962	*Once a Mouse. . .*	Marcia Brown	(398.2 Br)
1963	*The Snowy Day*	Ezra Jack Keats	(Ke)
1964	*Where the Wild Things Are*	Maurice Sendak	(Se)
1965	*May I Bring a Friend?*	Beni Montresor	(811 DeR)
1966	*Always Room for One More*	Nonny Hogrogian	(398.2 Ni)
1967	*Sam, Bangs and Moonshine*	Evaline Ness	(Ne)
1968	*Drummer Hoff*	Barbara Emberley	(398.2 Dr)
1969	*The Fool of the World and the Flying Ship*	Uri Shulevitz	(398.2 Ra)
1970	*Sylvester and the Magic Pebble*	William Steig	(St)
1971	*A Story, A Story*	Gail Haley	(398.2 Ha)
1972	*One Fine Day*	Nonny Hogrogian	(Ho)

CALDECOTT AWARD BOOKS

Year	Title	Illustrator	Call Number
1973	*The Funny Little Woman*	Blair Lent	(398.2 Mo)
1974	*Duffy and the Devil*	Margot Zemach	(398.2 Ze)
1975	*Arrow to the Sun*	Gerald McDermott	(398.2 McD)
1976	*Why Mosquitoes Buzz in People's Ears*	Leo and Diane Dillon	(398.2 Aa)
1977	*Ashanti to Zulu: African Traditions*	Leo and Diane Dillon	(398.2 Mu)
1978	*Noah's Ark*	Peter Spier	(Sp)
1979	*The Girl Who Loved Wild Horses*	Paul Goble	(Go)
1980	*Ox-Cart Man*	Barbara Cooney	(Ha)
1981	*Fables*	Arnold Lobel	(Lo)
1982	*Jumanji*	Chris Van Allsburg	(Va)
1983	*Shadow*	Marcie Brown	(841 Ce)
1984	*Glorious Flight: Across the Channel with Louis Bleroit*	Alice and Martin Provensen	(629.13 Pr)
1985	*Saint George and the Dragon*	Trina Schart Hyman	(398.2 Ho)
1986	*The Polar Express*	Chris Van Allsburg	(Va)
1987	*Hey, Al!*	Arthur Yorinks	(Yo)
1988	*Owl Moon*	Jane Yolen	(Yo)
1989	*Song and Dance Man*	Stephen Gammell	(Ac)
1990	*Lon Po Po: A Red-Riding Hood Story From China*	Ed Young	(398.2 Yo)

TITLE PAGE

It is interesting to know some things about a book before we read it.
The title page, which is near the front of the book, tells us many interesting
things. To locate these items, always use as many clue words as possible.

Winnie the Pooh

by

Alan Milne

Pictures by

E. H. Shepard

E. P. Dutton and
Company

New York

1954

TITLE - what the book is called -
Clue: Usually in large or dark letters

AUTHOR - the person who wrote the
book -
Clues: by, story by, written by, words
by, retold by

ILLUSTRATOR - the person who drew
the pictures -
Clues: pictures by, illustrated by,
drawings by

PUBLISHER - the printer who made
the book -
Clue: near the place of publication

PLACE OF PUBLICATION - where the
book was made -
Clue: usually a city or state

COPYRIGHT DATE - date when the
book was published, gives the right to
make copies -
Clue: numbers, usually located on
back of title page

HELPFUL HINTS!

Sometimes a picture is also included on the title page. Also, if you are looking
for the copyright date, don't forget to check the back of the title page.

Name ——————————— Grade ———————

TITLE PAGE

Write these things about a book you choose.

_____

Title

_____

_____

Author

_____

Illustrator

_____

Publisher

_____

Place of Publication

TITLE PAGE

FRECKLE
JUICE

by
Judy Blume

Illustrated by
Sonia O. Lisker

Four Winds Press/New York

Answer the following questions using the sample title page above.

Remember to look for clues to help you!

1. What is the title of the book? _____

2. Who is the author of the book? _____

3. Where was the book published? _____

4. Who is the illustrator? _____

5. Who is the publisher of the book? _____

6. Where could you look to find the copyright date of this book?

_____

TABLE OF CONTENTS

The table of contents is always found in the front of a book on a page or two after the title page.

It lists the units or chapters of the book and the page where they begin. It is arranged in the order they are printed from the beginning of the book to the end.

The table of contents of a nonfiction book is useful for finding a place where you can get information on a subject that might be included in the book.

The table of contents of a fiction book is useful for finding some things that happen in the story and to help you decide if you wish to read the book.

EXERCISE

Use this table of contents from the book, *Things To Do With Water* by Illa Podendorf.

Contents

Answer the following questions using the Table of Contents.

1. On what page would you look for information about water and color?

   _____

2. On what page would you look for information about water measurement?

   _____

3. On what page would you look for information about the temperature of water?

   _____

Name _____ Grade _____

THE PARTS OF A BOOK

ANSWERS:

title page	author	cover
copyright date	illustrator	spine
publisher	place of publication	title
	table of contents	

DIRECTIONS: Fill in the blank with the correct word.

1. The name of the book is the _____

2. The _____ writes the book.

3. The one who draws the pictures is the _____

4. The _____ protects the pages of the book.

5. The _____ holds the pages of the book together.

6. The company that prints or makes the book is called the _____

7. The page that tells the title, author , and publisher is the _____

_____

8. The year the book was published is the _____

9. The city where the book is made is called the _____

10. A list of chapters or stories arranged in the order in which they appear in the book is the _____

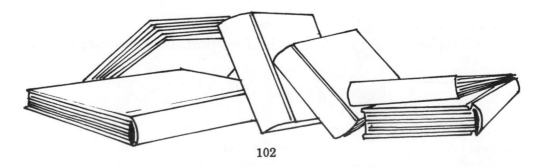

ARRANGEMENT OF FICTION BOOKS

Long, imaginary, made-up stories are called fiction. Fiction books are arranged on the shelf according to the author letters. The author letters are made from the first two letters of the author's last name. These letters are the book's call number, or address, because they tell where the book belongs on the shelf. An example of this would be Don Freeman - Author Letters - Fr.

A make believe shelf of fiction books might look like this in your library:

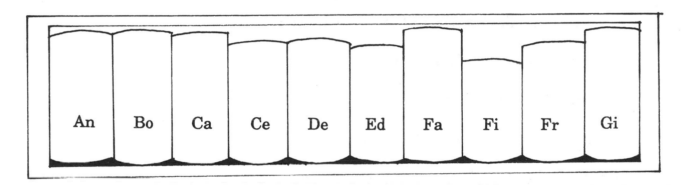

An | Bo | Ca | Ce | De | Ed | Fa | Fi | Fr | Gi

Test your brain! Pretend you are the author of a fiction book.

What would your author letters be?_____ (Remember that the author letters are made from the first two letters of the author's last name.)

ARRANGEMENT OF FICTION BOOKS

Write the call numbers in alphabetical order on the spaces below.

Pr	De	Mo	Ar	Sc	Lo	Ha	Br	Te	Kr

___ ___ ___ ___ ___ ___ ___ ___ ___ ___

Circle the call number for these fiction books.

1. *Curious George* by H. A. Rey

2. *Space Witch* by Don Freeman

3. *Harry the Dirty Dog* by Gene Zion

4. *Charlie Brown's All-Stars* by Charles Schulz

5. *Danny and the Dinosaur* by Syd Hoff

6. *Where the Wild Things Are* by Maurice Sendak

7. *Blaze and the Mountain Lion* by C. W. Anderson

8. *Tough Enough* by Ruth Carroll

9. *Flat Stanley* by Jeff Brown

10. *Miss Nelson is Missing!* by Harry Allard

Put the call numbers that you circled above in the order as they would appear on the shelf.

1._____   2._____   3._____   4._____   5._____

6._____   7._____   8._____   9_____   10._____

Name _____ Grade _____

ARRANGEMENT

of

FICTION BOOKS

The fiction book I selected today is

_____
Title

by _____
Author

The call number is _____
Letters

The spine of the book looks like this.

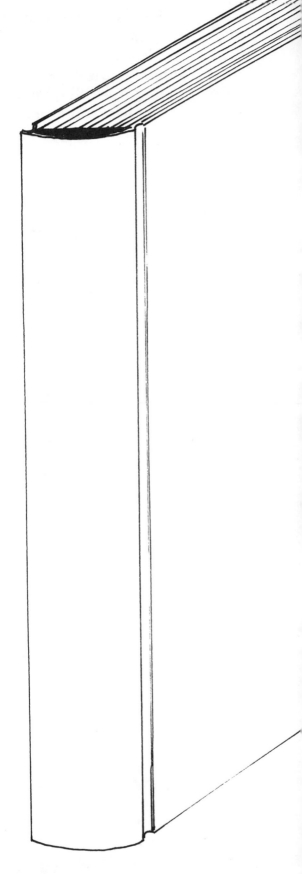

ARRANGEMENT OF NONFICTION BOOKS

Books that have information about different subjects are nonfiction. Folktales, fairy tales, poetry, and short stories are also nonfiction.

Nonfiction books are marked with a Dewey Call Number on their spines. The subject of the book determines the call number. The books are arranged on the shelf by the call number beginning with the lowest call number and working to the highest call number. Look at the example given:

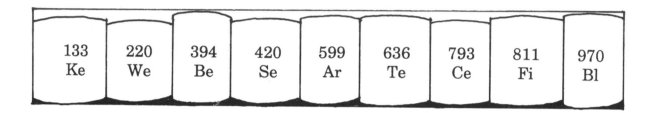

When there is more than one book with the same call number, then we use the author letters (as we did with fiction books.) Until we come to a larger number. Look at the example below.

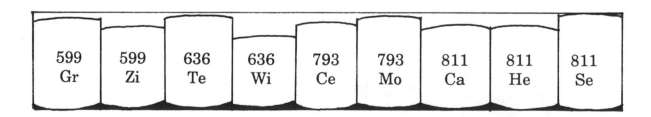

ARRANGEMENT OF NONFICTION BOOKS

Decide which call numbers would come first on a nonfiction shelf. Rewrite and arrange them in in the proper order.

1.
812	582	301	299	921	423	173
Ma	Be	Fr	Ho	Li	We	Mi

_____ _____ _____ _____ _____ _____ _____

2.
796	796	796	796	796	796	796
Me	Br	Dr	Mo	Tr	Ke	Re

_____ _____ _____ _____ _____ _____ _____

3.
599	598	523	551	582	501	572
Gl	Li	Ge	Sa	Zi	Lo	Mo

_____ _____ _____ _____ _____ _____ _____

Name _____ Grade _____

ARRANGEMENT

OF

NONFICTION BOOKS

The nonfiction book I selected today is

_____
Title

by _____
Author

The call number is _____
Numbers and letters

The spine of the book looks like this.

Bear books are
the best.

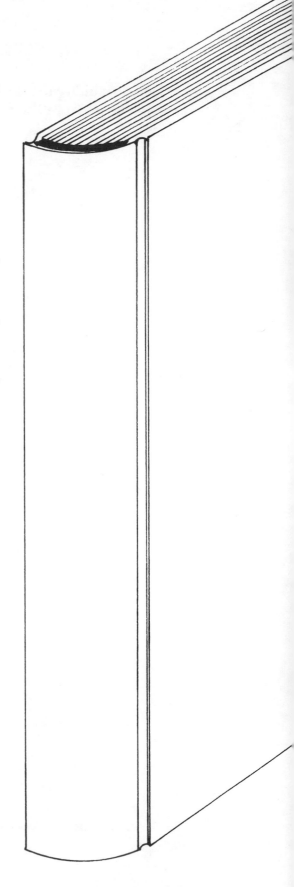

Name _____ Grade _____

ARRANGEMENT OF FICTION AND NONFICTION BOOKS

1. Arrange the nonfiction call numbers in the correct order.

582	811	636	919	582	394
Ud	Fi	Te	Ma	Mo	Wa

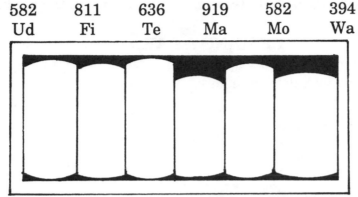

2. Arrange the fiction call numbers in the correct order.

Le	Am	Za	Te	Bu	Ab

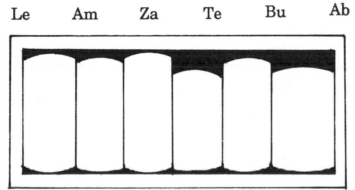

3. Separate these fiction and nonfiction call numbers and arrange them on the proper shelves in correct order.

793		525	398			423	
Ce	Be	Sh	Gr	St	We	Ea	Pa

Fiction   **Nonfiction**

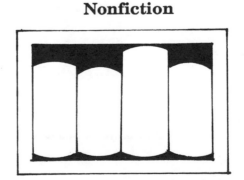

109

THE CARD CATALOG

The card catalog has cards for all the materials that are found in the library. It is a file of cards arranged in alphabetical order, much like a dictionary or index. It is in a special cabinet of drawers.

The information on the cards for books is the same as that on the title page of the book. There is also more information on the card that helps you to find the book on the shelf and to decide whether you want to choose the book.

READING A CARD

The information on a card is always placed in the same way.
Read and study the sample card below.

Mi	Milne, Alan
Call	**Author**
Number	

Winnie-the-Pooh
Title

E.H. Shepart	Dutton
Illustrator	**Publisher**

1954
Copyright date

158p
Pages

Gr. 2-3
Grade Level

THE CARD CATALOG

There are clues that help you to read the card (correctly).

CALL NUMBER

The call number is on the left side of the card all by itself. For nonfiction books, the call number has both numbers and letters. For fiction books, the call number has only letters. The call number tells you where the book is placed on the shelf. You need to know the call number to find the book.

AUTHOR

The author's name is turned around with the last name in front. A comma between the names is a clue to the author's name.

TITLE

The title is printed with mostly small letters and has a period at the end. You need to know the title to find the book on the shelf.

ILLUSTRATOR

The illustrator always comes after the title.

PUBLISHER

The publisher comes next. It is usually in a short form. It is always before the date.

COPYRIGHT DATE

The copyright date follows the publisher. It is the year the book was published.

PAGES AND GRADE LEVEL

Other information on the card is clued with an abbreviation. For example, p means pages, illus means illustrations and Gr. means grade level.

Some cards have an annotation which tells something about what is in the book or what the story is about. It can be used to help you decide whether to choose the book.

THE CARD CATALOG

The card catalog is used to locate materials in the library.

USING THE CARD CATALOG

The guide letters on the front of each drawer help you to decide which drawer to use.

The guide words inside each drawer that stand above the cards help you to get close to the place you are hunting. They are used like the guide words of a dictionary.

There are particular ways to look for certain things.

1. Look for the *last* name of an author

2. Look for the *first* word of a *title*, except The, A, and An.

3. Spell the subject correctly.

FINDING A BOOK

To find a book, you need to know the call number and title of the book because this is what you see when you go to the shelf.

You also need to decide if the book is fiction or nonfiction. You must also know the grade level so that you can go to the correct area of the library to start looking for your book

Remember: Fiction call numbers have only letters.
Nonfiction call numbers have both numbers and letters.

PRACTICE EXERCISE

Read the card together with the librarian. Put the information in the correct places on the blank card.

Call Number	Author
	Title
	Illustrator Publisher
	Copyright Date
	Pages
	Grade Level

PRACTICE EXERCISE

Name _____ Grade _____

Using a card catalog drawer, find a book card which is a plain colored card, read it, and complete the card.

Call Number	Author
	Title
	Illustrator Publisher
	Copyright Date
	Pages
	Grade Level

THE CARD CATALOG

THE SUBJECT CARD

Most people look for a subject or what they want the book to be about.

To do this, look for the subject on the top line of a card. It is printed in all capital letters. This is a clue to finding it.

When looking for a subject, know the correct spelling.

Then find the drawer with the first letter of the subject.

Inside the drawer, look at the guide words that stand above the cards. Decide where the subject would come between them, much as you would look for a word in the dictionary.

Next, look at the top line of each card between the guide cards. The cards are in alphabetical order, much like an index. Keep spelling the subject and find it.

When you have found the card you are looking for, read it and get the information you need.

EXERCISE

Cut on the dotted lines. Remove the slip of paper and follow the directions. Use what you have learned. Find the book on the shelf. Place this slip of paper in it and put them at the collection place.

- -

Name _____ Grade _____

Choose a book from the card catalog to locate in the library.

_____   _____
Call   Title
Number

_____   _____
Fiction or Nonfiction   Grade Level

- -

EXERCISE

Cut on the dotted line. Remove the slip of paper and follow the directions. Write the information you need to find the book. Find the book on the shelf. Place this slip of paper in it and put them at the collection place.

- -

Name _____ Grade _____

Choose a book with this subject to locate in the library.

_____
Subject

_____   _____
Call   Title
Number

_____   _____
Fiction or Nonfiction   Grade Level

THE CARD CATALOG

Decide in which drawer you would find these subjects.

A - C	G - H	N - P
D - F	I - M	Q - Z

1. DOGS _____

2. SCHOOL STORIES _____

3. HORSES _____

4. DINOSAURS _____

5. MYSTERY AND DETECTIVE STORIES _____

6. CATS _____

7. BICYCLES _____

8. PLANETS _____

Name _____ Grade _____

THE CARD CATALOG

This is a subject card. Answer the questions using this card.

```
                    BIRDS

   598.2           Darby, Gene
   Da                What is a Bird? Illus. by Lucy Hawkinson.
                   Benefic Press 1960
                     48p illus


                   Gr. 2-3
```

1. Subject   _____

2. Author   _____

3. Title   _____

4. Illustrator   _____

5. Call Number   _____

6. Grade Level   _____

7. Publisher   _____

8. Copyright Date   _____

9. Number of pages   _____

REFERENCE BOOKS

Reference books have a special purpose in the library. They are shelved in a special section of the library. They are used to get information for a report, to find an answer to a question or to read about something in which you are interested.

A dictionary, a thesaurus, and an encyclopedia are examples of reference books.

The call number of a reference book has a capital "R" as part of it. This tells you that it is shelved in the reference section.

These books usually have a colored sign-out card. This tells you that borrowing is limited. Check with your librarian and teacher for the rules in your library.

ENCYCLOPEDIA

An encyclopedia is a set of books that contain information about many different subjects. Because the amount of information cannot all be put into one book, it is divided into many smaller books. Each book is called a volume.

The volumes in each set are arranged in alphabetical order to make it easy to find the information. They are also numbered to make it easy to keep them in order on the shelf.

On the pages, the subjects are arranged in alphabetical order with guide words on each page like a dictionary.

FINDING INFORMATION

To find a subject, look for the letter it begins with and choose that volume. Then spell the subject correctly and use the guide words to find it as you would do in a dictionary. The subjects are usually printed with large, dark letters.

To find a person, look for the person's last name.

To find a place named with two parts, look for the first part.

REFERENCE BOOKS

USING GUIDE LETTERS

Below is a make-believe set of encyclopedias. Decide in which volume you would find the subjects listed. Write the guide letters in the blank space beside each subject.

A	B	C	D	E-F	G	H	I-J-K	L	M	N	O	P-Q	R	S	T	U-V	W	X-Y-Z	INDEX
1	2	3	4	5	6	7	8	9	10	11	12	13	14	15	16	17	18	19	20

1. Horses _____

2. Trees _____

3. Daniel Boone _____

4. Elephants _____

5. New York _____

6. Laura Ingalls Wilder _____

7. Dogs _____

8. Mountains _____

9. Pennsylvania _____

10. Snakes _____

TAKING NOTES

The reason you found information is to take notes. Do not copy from the encyclopedia. Instead, pick out key words and write short phrases. Later you can use them to write your own sentences, adding the words you need to make complete sentences.

GIVING THE SOURCE

It is important to tell where you got your information. It gives credit to the person who first wrote it. It also proves that you are correct.

The information which you read is called an article. It has a title.

The encyclopedia is a set. It has a name.

The volume you are using has certain letters. You are reading certain pages.

Name _____ Grade _____

ENCYCLOPEDIA

Find a subject which your are assigned. Write it on the line below.

SUBJECT ASSIGNED _____

Write some information about the subject. Do not copy from the article. Instead, write some key words in short phrases. Later you can use them to write your own sentences for a report.

_____

_____

_____

_____

_____

Tell where you found it by filling in the blanks below.

1. The title of the article is the heading of what you will read. It is usually in darker print on the page of the encyclopedia.

2. The encyclopedia is the name on the cover.

3. The volume is the letter on the spine.

4. The pages are the ones you will read.

Source of information

1. _____   2. _____
      Title of the Article   Encyclopedia

3. _____   4. _____
        Volume   Pages

MY FAVORITE BOOKS

1. _____
                                    Title

   _____   _____
   Call Number   Author

2. _____
                                    Title

   _____   _____
   Call Number   Author

3. _____
                                    Title

   _____   _____
   Call Number   Author

4. _____
                                    Title

   _____   _____
   Call Number   Author

5. _____
                                    Title

   _____   _____
   Call Number   Author

6. _____
                                    Title

   _____   _____
   Call Number   Author

7. _____
                                    Title

   _____   _____
   Call Number   Author

8. _____
                                    Title

   _____   _____
   Call Number   Author